Beginners Guide for Importing Goods to GCC Countries

Ahed ElMoarkache

Dedicated To My Beloved Family

Copyright © 2024 ColorCraft Adventures

All rights reserved. No part of this publication may be reproduced, distributed, or transmitted in any form or by any means, including photocopying, recording, or other electronic or mechanical methods, without the prior written permission of the publisher, except in the case of brief quotations embodied in critical reviews and certain other noncommercial uses permitted by copyright law.

Preface

In today's globalized economy, international trade is more accessible and more essential than ever. The Gulf Cooperation Council (GCC) countries, comprising Saudi Arabia, Kuwait, the United Arab Emirates, Qatar, Bahrain, and Oman, represent a dynamic and rapidly growing market. Their strategic location, robust economic policies, and significant consumer demand make them an attractive destination for businesses looking to import goods.

"Beginners Guide for Importing Goods to GCC Countries" is crafted with the novice importer in mind, but it offers valuable insights and practical knowledge that can benefit seasoned traders as well. The aim of this book is to demystify the complex world of international trade, making it approachable and manageable for everyone, from budding entrepreneurs to established business owners.

This book provides a structured, step-by-step approach to importing goods into the GCC. Each chapter delves into a critical aspect of the import process, ensuring that you gain a thorough understanding of what it takes to succeed in this field. From grasping the fundamentals of international trade to navigating the intricate customs regulations of each GCC country, this guide is your comprehensive companion on this journey.

Key Highlights:

Understanding the GCC Market: An overview of the economic landscape, trade policies, and market opportunities in the GCC countries.

Legal and Regulatory Framework: Detailed information on the legal requirements and regulatory standards for importing goods into the GCC.

Logistics and Supply Chain Management: Insights into managing the logistics of international trade, including shipping, warehousing, and distribution.

Customs Procedures: A guide to navigating the customs procedures and documentation required for importation.

Cultural and Business Practices: An exploration of the cultural nuances and business etiquette that can impact your success in the GCC market.

Throughout this book, you will find practical tips, real-world examples, and expert advice that will equip you with the knowledge and confidence to navigate the complexities of importing goods into the GCC.

Title: Beginners Guide for Importing Goods to GCC Countries

This outline provides a structured approach to creating a book on importing cargo for beginners. Each chapter covers a critical aspect of the import process, offering readers a step-by-step guide to becoming proficient in international trade.

Outlines:

Introduction

Welcome to the world of international trade! This book is designed to provide you with a comprehensive understanding of the process of importing cargo in GCC Countries. Whether you're a budding entrepreneur, a business owner looking to expand, or simply curious about how the GCC market operates, this guide will walk you through the essentials of importing goods from start to finish.

Chapter 1: The Basics of Importing

Understanding What Importing Is

The Benefits of Importing for Your Business

Key Terms and Definitions

What Are the GCC Countries'

Chapter 2: Planning Your Import Business

Researching the Market

Identifying Potential Products

Analyzing the Competition

Chapter 3: Legal and Regulatory Framework

Navigating Customs Regulations

GCC Import Licenses and Permits

Dealing with Import Tariffs and Taxes

Chapter 4: Sourcing Your Products

Finding Reliable Suppliers

Evaluating Product Quality

Negotiating Terms and Prices

Chapter 5: Shipping and Logistics

Choosing the Right Mode of Transport

Understanding Shipping Terms (Incoterms)

Tracking Your Shipment

Chapter 6: Financial Considerations

Budgeting for Your Imports

Financing Options for Importers

Chapter 7: Case Studies and Real-World Examples

Success Stories of Import Businesses

Common Challenges and Solutions

Lessons Learned from Experienced Importers

Conclusion

Useful Resources and Websites

Chapter 1: The Basics of Importing

Understanding What Importing Is

Importing is a fundamental aspect of international trade. It involves bringing goods or services into a country from abroad. Here's a brief overview to help you understand the **Concept:**

What are Imports? Imports are goods or services purchased in one country that were produced in another. They are essential components of international trade and contribute to a country's economy by providing access to products that may not be available domestically.

Benefits of Importing: By importing, a country can access goods that it cannot produce on its own, which can include everything from raw materials to finished products. This not only fulfills the demand for these goods but also helps in forming positive trade relationships with exporting countries.

Regulation of Imports: In the U.S., for example, imports and exports are overseen by Customs and Border Protection (CBP), which enforces regulations and tariffs associated with all products shipped into or out of the country. Other agencies like the FDA, EPA, and CDC may also be involved depending on the nature of the goods.

In the Gulf Cooperation Council (GCC) countries, imports and exports are regulated by a unified set of policies known as the GCC Common Customs Law. Here are some key points about the regulation of imports and exports in the GCC:

Customs Regulations: Goods destined for the GCC's mainland are subject to duty under the GCC's Common Customs Law, while goods destined for Free Trade Zones (FTZs) are exempt from duty.

Movement of Goods: Goods can be moved intra-GCC Customs Offices, which allows the passage of foreign goods from one member state to another without duplicate payment of customs duties at the destination country.

Duty Exemptions: Re-exports from UAE FTZs to third market destinations beyond the GCC Customs Zones are exempted from any duty. However, a deposit or guarantee equivalent to the applicable tariff amount on the goods is secured in lieu of customs duty for goods imported with the intention of re-exporting them.

Customs Authority: The Federal Customs Authority and the individual customs offices of the member states are responsible for the enforcement of these regulations1.

These regulations aim to facilitate trade and economic integration among the GCC countries while ensuring compliance with international trade laws. For more detailed information, you can refer to the official documents provided by the GCC Secretariat General or the customs authorities of the respective GCC member states.

Importing Process: The process typically involves declaring the goods to customs, providing necessary documentation, and paying any applicable duties and taxes. The exact regulations and required documents can vary depending on the country and the type of goods being imported

The Benefits of Importing for Your Business

Importing can offer a multitude of benefits for businesses, enhancing their competitiveness and growth potential.

Here are some key advantages:

Access to a Wider Range of Products: Importing allows businesses to offer a diverse array of products that may not be available locally, meeting consumer demands and preferences.

Cost Reduction: By sourcing goods from countries where production costs are lower, businesses can reduce their overall manufacturing expenses, leading to potentially higher profit margins.

Quality Improvement: Importing high-quality goods that are not produced domestically can enhance the quality of offerings, which can lead to customer satisfaction and loyalty.

Market Expansion: Engaging in international trade by importing goods can open up new markets for businesses, increasing sales and the potential for business growth.

Access to New Technologies: Importing can provide businesses with access to the latest technologies and innovations that are not yet available in their home market.

Economic Benefits: Importing can contribute to the national economy by providing consumers with a wider range of goods and services, which can stimulate consumer spending and economic growth.

These benefits highlight the strategic importance of importing in the global business landscape, enabling companies to stay competitive and responsive to market needs.

Key Terms and Definitions

Understanding key terms and definitions is crucial when dealing with the importation of goods.

Here are some essential terms you should be familiar with:

Bill of Lading (B/L): A Bill of Lading (B/L) is a crucial document in the shipping and freight industry, serving as a receipt for shipped goods, a contract between the shipper and carrier, and a document of title. There are various types of Bills of Lading, each serving different purposes and containing specific details pertinent to the shipment. Understanding these different types is essential for anyone involved in importing goods, especially in complex markets like the GCC countries.

Types of Bills of Lading

1. **Straight Bill of Lading:**

Purpose: This type is non-negotiable and made out to a specific consignee.

Usage: Commonly used when the goods have already been paid for or are being shipped between trusted parties.

Key Feature: Cannot be transferred or assigned to another party.

2. Order Bill of Lading:

Purpose: A negotiable instrument that can be endorsed to another party.

Usage: Often used when the payment for goods is secured through a letter of credit or when goods are being sold while in transit.

Key Feature: Can be transferred multiple times, facilitating trade.

3. Bearer Bill of Lading:

Purpose: Transferable by delivery, meaning whoever holds the bill has the right to claim the goods.

Usage: Less common due to the security risks involved but useful in some specific trade situations.

Key Feature: Possession of the document equates to ownership of the goods.

4. Clean Bill of Lading:

Purpose: Indicates that the goods were received in good condition without any apparent defects or damages.

Usage: Preferred by buyers and banks in letter of credit transactions because it assures them of the condition of the goods.

Key Feature: Does not note any discrepancies or issues with the cargo.

5. Claused Bill of Lading:

Purpose: Indicates that there is a problem with the cargo, such as damage or missing items.

Usage: Signals the buyer and the financial institutions of potential issues with the shipment.

Key Feature: Contains specific clauses or notations about the cargo's condition.

6. On-Board Bill of Lading:

Purpose: Confirms that the goods have been loaded onto the vessel.

Usage: Often required in letter of credit transactions as proof of shipment.

Key Feature: Specifies the date and the vessel on which the goods were loaded.

7. Received for Shipment Bill of Lading:

Purpose: Indicates that the carrier has received the goods but they have not yet been loaded onto the ship.

Usage: Used when there is a delay between the receipt of goods and their loading onto the vessel.

Key Feature: Not as conclusive as an On-Board Bill of Lading for confirming shipment.

8. Through Bill of Lading:

Purpose: Covers the transportation of goods across multiple carriers or different modes of transport (e.g., from sea to land).

Usage: Useful for complex logistics chains involving multiple legs of a journey.

Key Feature: Details the entire journey from origin to final destination.

9. Multimodal or Combined Transport Bill of Lading:

Purpose: Similar to a Through Bill of Lading, it covers goods transported via multiple modes (e.g., sea, rail, truck).

Usage: Ideal for international shipments requiring diverse transportation methods.

Key Feature: Provides a single document for the entire transportation process.

10. Direct Bill of Lading:

Purpose: Used when there is a direct shipment from the exporter to the importer without intermediaries.

Usage: Simplifies the documentation when no transshipment or intermediary handling is involved.

Key Feature: Typically used for straightforward, uncomplicated shipping routes.

11. Conclusion

Each type of Bill of Lading serves a specific purpose and provides different benefits and protections depending on the nature of the transaction and the requirements of the parties involved. For importers in GCC countries, understanding these distinctions is vital to ensure smooth, efficient, and secure transactions. This knowledge helps in selecting the right type of Bill of Lading for your specific needs, thereby mitigating risks and facilitating successful international trade.

Commercial Invoice (CI): A Commercial Invoice is a critical document in international trade, serving multiple purposes in the transaction process between a buyer and a seller. It acts as a record of the sale, a customs declaration, and a key document for accounting and payment purposes.

Here's a detailed explanation of what a Commercial Invoice is, its functions, and its key components:

Definition

A Commercial Invoice is a formal document issued by the exporter (seller) to the importer (buyer) that outlines the terms of the sale and provides detailed information about the goods being sold. It is used primarily for customs clearance, accounting, and payment processes.

Functions of a Commercial Invoice

1. Customs Declaration:

The Commercial Invoice is used by customs authorities to determine the value of the goods for the assessment of duties and taxes. It provides essential details about the nature, value, and quantity of the goods, ensuring proper classification and taxation.

2. Proof of Sale:

It serves as an official record of the sale agreement between the exporter and the importer. It documents the terms of sale, including the price, shipping terms, and payment conditions.

3. Accounting and Payment:

For both the exporter and the importer, the Commercial Invoice is a key accounting document. It records the financial aspects of the transaction and is used to process payments through banks or other financial institutions.

4. Shipment Tracking:

The invoice often includes details about the shipment, such as the method of transport and tracking numbers, which help both parties monitor the delivery status.

Key Components of a Commercial Invoice

Exporter and Importer Details:

Names, addresses, and contact information of both the seller (exporter) and the buyer (importer).

5. Invoice Number and Date:

A unique invoice number for reference and the date of issue.

6. Description of Goods:

Detailed description of the goods being sold, including quantity, weight, dimensions, and any identifying marks or numbers.

7. Unit Price and Total Price:

The unit price of each item and the total price of the entire shipment. This should include the currency in which the transaction is made.

8. Terms of Sale (Incoterms):

Specifies the agreed-upon Incoterms (International Commercial Terms), such as FOB (Free On Board), CIF (Cost, Insurance, and Freight), or DDP (Delivered Duty

Paid), which define the responsibilities of each party regarding shipping, insurance, and tariffs.

9. Payment Terms:

Conditions under which the payment will be made, including the payment method (e.g., letter of credit, wire transfer) and the due date for payment.

10. Shipping Details:

Information about the shipment, including the mode of transport (e.g., air, sea, land), the name of the carrier, the port of loading, the port of discharge, and the final destination.

11. Customs Information:

Harmonized System (HS) codes for the goods, which help customs authorities classify the items correctly. It may also include information on the country of origin and any relevant import/export licenses or certificates.

12. Signature:

The invoice should be signed by an authorized representative of the exporter, validating the document's authenticity.

13. Importance in International Trade

The Commercial Invoice is indispensable in international trade for several reasons:

Facilitates Customs Clearance: By providing detailed information about the goods and their value, it helps expedite the customs clearance process, reducing delays and potential penalties.

14. Ensures Accurate Payment:

It serves as a reference for both parties to ensure that the correct amount is paid and received, based on the agreed-upon terms.

15. Legal Protection:

As a legal document, it protects both the buyer and the seller by clearly outlining the terms of the sale and the expectations of both parties.

16. Record Keeping:

It aids in maintaining accurate financial records for accounting, tax purposes, and future reference.

In summary, the Commercial Invoice is a vital document that underpins the efficiency and legality of international trade transactions. Its detailed and accurate completion is essential for smooth business operations, compliance with customs regulations, and effective financial management.

Certificate of Origin (COO):

Certificate of Origin: Definition and Importance

A **Certificate of Origin (CO)** is an essential document in international trade that certifies the country in which the goods being shipped were manufactured. It is a critical piece of documentation used by customs authorities to determine the eligibility of the goods for import tariffs, trade agreements, and other regulatory requirements.

Functions of a Certificate of Origin

1. **Verification of Origin:**

- The primary function of a CO is to verify the country of origin of the goods. This helps customs authorities in the importing country determine whether the goods qualify for preferential tariff rates or are subject to any import restrictions.

2. **Compliance with Trade Agreements:**

- Many countries have bilateral or multilateral trade agreements that provide reduced tariffs or duty-free treatment for goods originating from the partner countries. A CO is necessary to claim these benefits under agreements such as NAFTA (North American Free Trade Agreement) or the EU's trade agreements.

3. **Customs Clearance:**

- Customs authorities use the CO to assess the goods accurately and to ensure compliance with local regulations. This document is crucial for the smooth and timely clearance of goods at the port of entry.

4. **Consumer Information:**
- For certain products, particularly those where the origin is associated with quality or specific characteristics (e.g., wines, cheeses), a CO provides assurance to consumers about the authenticity of the product's origin.

Types of Certificates of Origin

1. **Non-Preferential Certificate of Origin:**
- This type certifies that the goods do not qualify for any preferential treatment and are subject to standard tariffs. It is used when there are no special trade agreements between the exporting and importing countries.

2. **Preferential Certificate of Origin:**
- This type certifies that the goods qualify for reduced tariffs or duty-free entry under specific trade agreements. Examples include the EUR.1 certificate for European Union trade

agreements or the Form A for the Generalized System of Preferences (GSP).

Key Components of a Certificate of Origin

1. **Exporter Details:**
- Name, address, and contact information of the exporter.

2. **Importer Details:**
- Name, address, and contact information of the importer.

3. **Description of Goods:**
- Detailed description of the goods, including HS codes, quantity, weight, and any identifying marks.

4. **Country of Origin:**
- The country where the goods were manufactured or produced.
-

5. **Declaration Statement:**
- A statement certifying the authenticity of the information provided, typically signed by the exporter or an authorized agent.

6. **Certification by Authorized Body:**

- The CO must be certified by an authorized body, such as a Chamber of Commerce or a trade association. This certification verifies that the document has been reviewed and is accurate.

7. **Date and Signature:**

- The date of issuance and the signature of the authorized official from the certifying body.

Importance in International Trade

1. **Eligibility for Preferential Tariffs:**

- A CO allows importers to take advantage of reduced tariffs or duty-free entry under various trade agreements, reducing the cost of imported goods.

2. **Regulatory Compliance:**

- Ensures that goods meet the regulatory requirements of the importing country, avoiding delays, fines, or rejection of the shipment.

3. **Trade Facilitation:**

Simplifies the customs clearance process by providing a clear and verified origin of the goods, ensuring faster processing times.

- **Legal Protection:**

Provides a legal document that can be used to resolve disputes over the origin of goods, protecting both the exporter and the importer.

- **Market Access:**

Certain markets have restrictions on goods from specific countries. A CO helps in verifying that the goods comply with the import regulations of the destination market.

Incoterms:

Incoterms, short for International Commercial Terms, are a set of standardized trade terms published by the International Chamber of Commerce (ICC) that define the responsibilities of sellers and buyers in international transactions. These terms clarify who is responsible for paying for and managing the shipment, insurance, documentation, customs clearance, and other logistical activities. By specifying these obligations, Incoterms help prevent misunderstandings and disputes in international trade.

Key Functions of Incoterms

1. **Clarifying Responsibilities:**

- Incoterms outline whether the buyer or seller is responsible for transportation costs, insurance, and handling of goods at various stages of transit.

2. **Defining Risk Transfer:**

- They specify the point at which the risk of loss or damage to the goods transfers from the seller to the buyer.

3. **Streamlining Transactions:**

- By providing clear terms, Incoterms facilitate smoother transactions and help in drafting sales contracts.

Categories of Incoterms

Incoterms are divided into two main categories based on the mode of transport:

1. **Incoterms for Any Mode of Transport:**
- These terms apply whether the goods are transported by sea, air, rail, or road.
- Examples: EXW, FCA, CPT, CIP, DAP, DPU, DDP.

2. **Incoterms for Sea and Inland Waterway Transport:**
- These terms are specifically used for goods transported over water.
- Examples: FAS, FOB, CFR, CIF.

Common Incoterms

1. **EXW (Ex Works):**
- The seller makes the goods available at their premises. The buyer bears all costs and risks involved in transporting the goods from there to the destination.

2. **FCA (Free Carrier):**
- The seller delivers the goods to a carrier or another person nominated by the buyer at the seller's premises or another named place. The buyer assumes all risks and costs from that point.

3. **CPT (Carriage Paid To):**
- The seller pays for the carriage of the goods up to the named place of destination. Risk transfers to the buyer when the goods are handed over to the carrier.

4. **CIP (Carriage and Insurance Paid To):**
- Similar to CPT, but the seller also pays for insurance against the buyer's risk of loss or damage during transit.

5. **DAP (Delivered at Place):**
- The seller delivers the goods to the named place of destination. The buyer is responsible for import duties and any further transport costs.

6. **DPU (Delivered at Place Unloaded):**

- The seller delivers and unloads the goods at the named place of destination. The buyer handles import clearance and any additional transportation costs.

7. **DDP (Delivered Duty Paid):**
- The seller bears all costs and risks of delivering the goods to the destination, including import duties and taxes. The buyer takes over only when the goods are ready for unloading.

8. **FAS (Free Alongside Ship):**
- The seller delivers the goods alongside the vessel at the named port of shipment. The buyer assumes all risks and costs from that point onward.

9. **FOB (Free on Board):**
- The seller loads the goods onto the vessel at the named port of shipment. Risk transfers to the buyer once the goods are on board.

10. **CFR (Cost and Freight):**
- The seller pays for the cost of freight to transport the goods to the named port of destination. The risk transfers to the buyer once the goods are loaded on the vessel.

11. **CIF (Cost, Insurance and Freight):**
- Similar to CFR, but the seller also provides insurance against the buyer's risk of loss or damage during the voyage.

    Tariff: A tax imposed by a government on goods or services imported from another country to protect domestic industries from foreign competition or to generate revenue.

    Customs Duty: A tariff or tax imposed on goods when transported across international borders, typically aimed at raising state revenue and protecting domestic industries.

    Free Trade Zone (FTZ): An area within a country where goods may be landed, handled, manufactured, or reconfigured without the intervention of the customs authorities.

Automated Export System (AES): The system used by U.S. exporters to electronically declare their international exports to the Census Bureau to help compile U.S. export and trade.

In the context of GCC customs, several key terms are essential to understand the customs processes and regulations. Here are some of the important terms and definitions:

The Gulf Cooperation Council (GCC), also known as the Cooperation Council for the Arab States of the Gulf, is a regional, intergovernmental, political, and economic union comprising six Middle Eastern countries: Bahrain, Kuwait, Oman, Qatar, Saudi Arabia, and the United Arab Emirates. The GCC was established in Riyadh, Saudi Arabia, in May 1981 with the goal of achieving unity among its members based on common objectives and similar political and cultural identities rooted in Arab and Islamic cultures.

Here are some key points about the GCC:

Purpose: The GCC aims to strengthen relations among its member countries and promote cooperation among their citizens. Its main objectives include economic coordination, security cooperation, and cultural exchange.

Leadership: The presidency of the council rotates annually, and the highest decision-making entity is the Supreme Council, consisting of GCC heads of state. Decisions of the Supreme Council require unanimous approval.

Military Arm: The Peninsula Shield Force serves as the military arm of the GCC, formed in 1984.

Agreements: The GCC has agreements related to security coordination (such as the creation of the Peninsula Shield Force) and economic coordination (including a customs union and value-added tax implementation)

Common Customs Law: The legal framework that governs customs procedures within the GCC states.

Harmonized System (HS): An internationally standardized system of names and numbers for classifying traded products used by customs authorities worldwide, including the GCC.

Customs Tariff: A schedule of duties imposed by a government on imported or in some countries exported goods.

Customs Duty: A tariff or tax on the importation and exportation of goods.

Free Zone: A designated region where goods are stored, handled, manufactured, or reconfigured and re-exported without the intervention of the customs authorities.

Temporary Admission: The process that allows goods to be brought into a customs territory conditionally relieved from payment of customs duties and taxes.

Re-exportation: The shipment of goods to a country from which they were previously imported, to be shipped out again to the original exporting country or to a third country.

Drawback: A refund of customs duties paid on imported goods which are subsequently exported.

Chapter 2: Planning Your Import Business

Researching the GCC Market

Researching the GCC market trends is essential for understanding the economic landscape and identifying opportunities for growth and investment. Here are some key trends in the GCC market:

Consulting Market Growth: The GCC consulting market is expected to expand by 11% and exceed $6 billion in revenue this year, driven by economic diversification strategies and mega projects1.

Construction Sector: The building and construction sector's growth is projected to drive the GCC calcium oxide market, which is expected to reach a market capitalization of $245.4 million by 2033.

Pharmaceuticals: The GCC generic drugs market is also showing significant growth opportunities, with detailed analysis available for each sub-segment and forecasts at the regional and country level from 2024-2032.

Economic Resilience: Despite global economic challenges, the GCC countries have shown remarkable resilience, with GDP growth expected to strengthen at 3.7% in 2024. This is supported by loosening OPEC+ oil production quotas and continued government investment in line with economic diversification goals.

Technology and Innovation: There is a trend towards establishing Centers of Excellence in areas such as artificial intelligence, cloud computing, engineering, data analytics, and cybersecurity. This is part of a broader move to transition from cost centers to profit centers, generating new revenue streams.

These trends indicate a dynamic and evolving GCC market, with various sectors poised for growth. Businesses and investors looking to enter or expand in the GCC market should consider these trends when making strategic decisions.

Identifying Potential Products

Identifying potential products for the Gulf Cooperation Council (GCC) market involves understanding the region's economic landscape, consumer preferences, and growth sectors. Based on recent data, here are some key areas that hold potential for product development and investment:

Green Growth Sectors: The GCC is focusing on diversifying its economy through green growth strategies. This includes renewable energy, green buildings, sustainable transport, water management, and waste management.

E-Commerce: The e-commerce market in the GCC is experiencing rapid growth, with a forecasted revenue of US$50 billion by 2025. This sector is supported by an increasing number of online shoppers and the rise of local and global e-commerce platforms.

Technology and Innovation: With the region's push towards modernization and digital transformation, there is a growing demand for innovative technological solutions and services.

Healthcare Products: The healthcare sector in the GCC is expanding, creating opportunities for pharmaceuticals, medical devices, and health-related technologies.

Food and Beverage: The GCC has a growing demand for high-quality food and beverage products, including organic and health-focused options.

Luxury Goods and Fashion: The region's affluent consumer base continues to drive demand for luxury items, designer clothing, and accessories.

Educational Services: There is a significant focus on education and training services to support the region's vision of a knowledge-based economy.

Tourism and Hospitality: With major events like Expo 2020 and the FIFA World Cup 2022, there's an increased interest in tourism-related products and services.

Construction and Infrastructure: Ongoing and upcoming mega-projects in the GCC call for construction materials, machinery, and related services.

Fintech: Financial technology products and services are gaining traction, with a focus on payment solutions, digital banking, and investment platforms.

These sectors represent just a snapshot of the diverse opportunities available in the GCC market. For businesses looking to enter or expand in the GCC, it's crucial to conduct thorough market research and understand the unique characteristics and requirements of each member country.

Analyzing the Competition

Analyzing the competition in GCC countries involves understanding the unique economic dynamics and regulatory environments of each member state. The GCC has been experiencing a shift towards more collaborative and strategic competition, particularly in light of recent geopolitical developments.

Here are some key points to consider when analyzing competition in the GCC:

Diverse Economic Agendas: Each GCC country has its own economic vision and development goals, which can lead to different competitive strategies and priorities.

Regulatory Frameworks: The emergence of competition law in the GCC is relatively recent. There is a discussion about the need for a uniform competition policy and law to regulate competition in the region, similar to that of the European Union.

Sector-Specific Trends: Competition varies significantly across different sectors. For instance, the energy sector may have different competitive dynamics compared to the retail or technology sectors.

Foreign Investment: The GCC countries are increasingly open to foreign investment, which adds another layer of competition as international companies enter the market.

Intra-Regional Trade: There is a trend of increasing intra-regional trade among GCC countries, which affects competition, especially in sectors like manufacturing and services.

Digital Transformation: The rapid digital transformation across the GCC is creating new opportunities and competitive landscapes, particularly in e-commerce and fintech.

Socio-Political Factors: The socio-political environment can influence competition, as seen in the recent rapprochement between GCC countries and Iran, which may lead to new economic collaborations and competitive scenarios.

Chapter 3: Legal and Regulatory Framework

Navigating Customs Regulations

Navigating customs regulations in the Gulf Cooperation Council (GCC) countries requires an understanding of the Common Customs Law that governs the import and export of goods within the region. Here are some key points to consider:

Common External Tariff (CET): The GCC applies a CET for products imported from outside the GCC, which means uniform customs duties across all member states.

Unified Customs Regulations: There are unified customs regulations and procedures to streamline the process of moving goods within the GCC.

Single Entry Point: Goods entering the GCC will have customs duties collected at the first point of entry, after which they can move freely within the member states1.

Prohibitions and Restrictions: Certain goods may be prohibited or restricted, so it's important to check the specific regulations for each type of product.

Customs Declarations: Importers must provide accurate customs declarations for the goods they are importing, including value, description, and origin.

Inspection of Goods: Customs authorities have the right to inspect goods to ensure compliance with regulations.

Payment of Duties: Importers are responsible for paying the appropriate customs taxes and duties before the release of goods.

Exemptions: There are cases where customs duties and taxes are suspended, such as goods in transit, re-exportation, and temporary admission.

Service Fees and Charges: Additional fees and charges may apply for customs services.

Customs Brokers: Engaging a licensed customs broker can facilitate the clearance process and ensure compliance with all regulations.

For detailed information on customs regulations in the GCC, you can refer to the official documents provided by the GCC Secretariat General or consult with legal experts who specialize in GCC trade law. It's also advisable to stay updated with any changes in the law, as the GCC countries continue to evolve their customs policies to support economic integration and development.

GCC Import Licenses and Permits

In the Gulf Cooperation Council (GCC) countries, obtaining import licenses and permits is a crucial step for businesses looking to import goods. The process and requirements can vary depending on the member state and the type of goods being imported. Here's a general overview of the steps and documentation needed:

Trade License: Companies must have a valid trade license from the Department of Economic Development (DED) in the respective emirate or GCC country.

Customs Registration: Businesses need to register with the customs authorities and obtain a customs code, which is essential for import transactions.

Import Permit: For restricted or duty-exempted goods, an import permit from the competent agencies is required.

Standard Trade Documentation: This includes a commercial invoice, certificate of origin, detailed packing list, bill of entry or airway bill, and any other required documents specific to the goods.

Health and Safety Certificates: For food products, an original health certificate and, if applicable, a Halal slaughter certificate are necessary.

Legalization of Documents: Non-food shipments require document legalization, which is a two-step process involving verification and submission to the UAE Embassy or Consulate1.

Agency Approvals: Depending on the goods, approvals and authorizations from relevant authorities may be needed. It's important to note that these are general guidelines and specific requirements can differ. For instance, free trade zones (FTZs) within the GCC may have different regulations compared to mainland areas. It's advisable to consult with local authorities or a customs broker to ensure compliance with all import regulations.

For the most accurate and up-to-date information, you should refer to the official websites of the customs and trade authorities in the GCC country where you plan to import goods.

Dealing with Import Tariffs and Taxes

Dealing with import tariffs and taxes in the Gulf Cooperation Council (GCC) countries involves understanding the Common Customs Law and the Unified Customs Tariff. Here are some key points to consider:

Harmonized System (HS) 2022: The GCC countries have adopted the HS 2022, which includes changes in tariff classification, introduction of new tariff codes, and amendments to the description of goods. It's important for businesses to review their customs classification procedures to ensure compliance.

Common External Tariff (CET): The GCC applies a CET for products imported from outside the GCC, which means uniform customs duties across all member states.

Product-Specific Tariffs: Some products may have higher tariffs, and items like tobacco, pork, and alcohol can have tariffs exceeding 100% in some GCC countries.

Exemptions and Suspensions: There are cases where customs duties and taxes are suspended, such as goods in transit, re-exportation, and temporary admission.

Service Fees and Charges: Additional fees and charges may apply for customs services.

VAT: The GCC countries have implemented Value Added Tax (VAT) at different rates, which is also applicable to imported goods.

Customs Declarations: Accurate customs declarations are crucial to avoid delays in customs clearance and potential fines or penalties.

Documentation: Ensure all required documentation is in order, including commercial invoices, certificates of origin, and packing lists.

Customs Brokers: Engaging a licensed customs broker can facilitate the clearance process and ensure compliance with all regulations.

For businesses, it's essential to stay updated with the latest customs regulations and tariff changes. Consulting with legal experts or customs brokers can provide valuable assistance in navigating the complexities of import tariffs and taxes in the GCC.

Chapter 4: Sourcing Your Products

Finding Reliable Suppliers

Finding reliable suppliers is a critical step in product sourcing. Here are some strategies to help you identify and partner with trustworthy suppliers:

Define Your Criteria: Establish clear standards for quality, cost, delivery time, and service.

Research: Utilize online marketplaces and B2B platforms to find potential suppliers. Look for reviews and ratings to gauge reliability.

Check Certifications: Ensure suppliers have relevant quality certifications like ISO or QS, which can be indicators of reliable operations.

Evaluate Financial Stability: Consider the supplier's financial health to reduce the risk of disruptions in your supply chain.

Assess Geo-Political Climate: Be aware of the political and economic stability in the supplier's region, as it can impact their reliability.

Order Samples: Before committing, order samples to assess the quality of the products firsthand.

Negotiate Terms: Clearly communicate your needs and expectations, and negotiate terms that benefit both parties.

Monitor Performance: After selecting a supplier, continuously monitor their performance and the quality of the deliveries.

Build Relationships: Developing a strong relationship with your suppliers can lead to better service and favorable terms in the long run.

By following these steps, you can increase your chances of finding suppliers that will meet your business needs and contribute to its success. Remember, thorough due diligence and ongoing evaluation are key to maintaining a strong supply chain.

Evaluating Product Quality

Evaluating product quality for import to GCC countries is a critical process that involves several steps to ensure compliance with the region's standards and regulations. Here's a general approach to evaluating product quality:

Understand GCC Standards: Familiarize yourself with the GCC standards for imported foods, which are based on international benchmarks like Codex, OIE, and IPPC.

Risk-Based Approach: The GCC employs a risk-based approach to food safety, which means that the evaluation of product quality will depend on the potential risks associated with the food item1.

Documentation and Certification: Ensure that the exporting country provides the necessary documentation and certification to assure the safety and suitability of the food shipments1.

Health and Safety Certificates: Obtain health certificates and, if applicable, Halal certifications for animal and plant health.

Food Inspection: Be prepared for food inspection by the competent authorities in the importing country to verify conformity to GCC technical regulations.

Supplier Compliance: Verify that your suppliers comply with the GCC's regulatory requirements and that they can consistently provide products that meet these standards.

Quality Control Systems: Implement quality control systems that align with GCC guidelines to monitor and maintain the quality of products throughout the supply chain.

Legalization of Documents: Ensure that all required documents are legalized appropriately, which involves verification and submission to the respective GCC country's embassy or consulate.

Product Testing: Conduct product testing as per GCC guidelines to ensure that the products meet the necessary quality and safety standards before shipment.

Continuous Monitoring: Continuously monitor product quality even after the initial evaluation to ensure ongoing compliance with GCC standards.

By following these steps and ensuring thorough documentation and compliance with GCC regulations, you can effectively evaluate and maintain the quality of products imported into GCC countries. It's also advisable to stay updated with any changes in the regulations, as the GCC countries continue to evolve their policies to support economic integration and development.

Negotiating Terms and Prices

Negotiating terms and prices for imports to GCC countries involves several considerations to ensure a successful transaction. Here are some strategies to help you negotiate effectively:

Understand the Market: Research the local market conditions, demand, and standard pricing for the products you're interested in importing.

Know the Regulations: Familiarize yourself with the GCC's import regulations, tariffs, and taxes to factor these into your cost calculations.

Cultural Awareness: Be mindful of the business culture in GCC countries, which values relationship-building and respect for local customs during negotiations.

Quality and Standards: Ensure the products meet GCC standards, which may influence the price and terms of the agreement.

Volume Discounts: If you're importing in large quantities, negotiate volume discounts or better terms.

Payment Terms: Discuss payment terms that are favorable to your cash flow, such as extended payment periods or installment plans.

Shipping and Handling: Clarify who will be responsible for shipping costs, insurance, and handling fees.

Currency Fluctuations: Consider the impact of currency exchange rates on the transaction and negotiate terms that protect against significant fluctuations.

Contract Clarity: Ensure all negotiated terms are clearly stated in the contract to avoid future disputes.

Legal Advice: Consult with legal experts familiar with GCC trade laws to review contracts and agreements.

Remember, successful negotiations often result from preparation, clear communication, and a willingness to find mutually beneficial solutions. It's also important to stay informed about any free trade agreements or economic partnerships that may impact trade negotiations with GCC countries.

Chapter 5: Shipping and Logistics

Choosing the Right Mode of Transport

Choosing the right mode of transport for importing goods to GCC countries is a crucial decision that can affect the efficiency and cost-effectiveness of your supply chain. Here are some factors to consider when selecting the mode of transport:

Type of Goods: The nature of the goods (perishable, fragile, bulky, etc.) will influence the choice of transport.

Cost: Compare the costs associated with different modes of transport, keeping in mind the total cost, including tariffs and taxes.

Speed: If time is a critical factor, air transport may be the best option, despite being more expensive.

Volume and Weight: For heavy and large shipments, sea or rail transport might be more suitable and cost-effective.

Distance: Long distances often favor sea transport due to lower costs, while shorter distances may benefit from the flexibility of road transport.

Safety and Reliability: Consider the safety record and reliability of the transport mode, especially for valuable or hazardous goods.

Environmental Impact: Some businesses may prioritize modes of transport with a lower **carbon footprint as part of their sustainability goals.**

Customs and Regulations: Familiarize yourself with the customs procedures and regulations for each mode of transport, as outlined in the GCC Unified Guide for Customs Procedures.

Infrastructure: Assess the availability and quality of infrastructure, such as ports, airports, and rail networks, in the origin and destination countries.

Multimodal Options: Sometimes, a combination of different modes of transport (intermodal transport) can offer the best balance of speed, cost, and reliability.

It's important to weigh these factors against your specific business needs and the requirements of the goods you're importing. Consulting with logistics experts and customs brokers can also provide valuable insights into making the best choice for your imports to GCC countries.

Understanding Shipping Terms (Incoterms)

Understanding Shipping Terms, or Incoterms, is essential for conducting international trade as they define the responsibilities of buyers and sellers in the export transaction. Incoterms are a set of 11 internationally recognized rules issued by the International Chamber of Commerce (ICC) which clarify the tasks, costs, and risks to be borne by buyers and sellers in these transactions.

Here's a brief overview of some commonly used Incoterms:

EXW (Ex Works): The seller makes the goods available at their premises. The buyer is responsible for all charges and risks involved in taking the goods from the seller's location to the destination.

FCA (Free Carrier): The seller delivers the goods, cleared for export, to the carrier chosen by the buyer at a specified location.

CPT (Carriage Paid To): The seller pays for the carriage of the goods up to the named place of destination.

CIP (Carriage and Insurance Paid To): Similar to CPT, but the seller also has to procure insurance against the buyer's risk of loss or damage to the goods during the carriage1.

DAP (Delivered at Place): The seller delivers when the goods are placed at the disposal of the buyer on the arriving means of transport ready for unloading at the named place of destination.

DPU (Delivered at Place Unloaded): The seller delivers the goods, and transfers risk, to the buyer when the goods are unloaded at the agreed place of destination.

DDP (Delivered Duty Paid): The seller delivers the goods cleared for import to the buyer at destination. The seller bears all costs and risks involved in bringing the goods to the place of destination.

These terms are standardized to prevent confusion in trade contracts. It's important to specify which version of Incoterms is being used in the contract, such as Incoterms 2020, to ensure clarity for all parties involved.

For a complete list and detailed explanation of all Incoterms, you can refer to the ICC's official documentation or consult with a trade expert.

Tracking Your Shipment

Tracking your shipment is a straightforward process that can be done through various methods provided by shipping companies. Here's how you can track your shipment:

Tracking Number: Use the tracking number provided by the shipping company. This number is unique to your shipment and can be used to track its status online.

Online Tracking: Visit the shipping company's website and enter your tracking number in their tracking tool to get real-time updates.

Mobile App: Many shipping companies have mobile apps that allow you to track your shipment on the go.

Customer Support: If you're unable to track your shipment online, you can contact the shipping company's customer support for assistance.

Text Updates: Some companies offer the option to receive text updates by sending a message with your tracking number to a designated number.

Email Tracking: You can also track by email, where you'll receive updates directly to your inbox.

Remember to keep your tracking number handy, as it's the key to accessing information about your shipment's journey. If you encounter any issues or delays, the shipping company's customer support is the best resource for assistance.

Chapter 6: Financial Considerations

Budgeting for Your Imports

In this chapter, we'll explore the financial aspects of importing goods into the GCC countries. Effective budgeting is crucial for the success of your import business. Here's what we'll cover:

Understanding Costs

Product Costs: The purchase price of the goods you're importing.

Shipping Costs: Includes freight, insurance, and handling fees.

Customs Duties: Tariffs imposed on imported goods by GCC customs authorities.

Taxes: Value-added tax (VAT) and other applicable taxes in the GCC.

Currency Exchange: Impact of exchange rates on your import costs.

Creating a Budget

Forecasting: Estimating future costs based on historical data and market research.

Allocating Funds: Setting aside money for each aspect of the import process.

Contingency Planning: Preparing for unexpected expenses or changes in costs.

Cost-Saving Strategies.

Bulk Purchasing: Negotiating discounts for larger orders.

Comparative Shopping: Finding the best prices and terms for products and shipping.

Optimizing Shipping: Choosing the most cost-effective shipping methods and routes.

Financial Tools and Resources

Currency Hedging: Protecting against unfavorable currency movements.

Trade Finance: Exploring options like letters of credit and trade loans.

Budgeting Software: Utilizing tools for tracking and managing your finances.

Case Studies of Real-world examples of successful budgeting strategies in the import business.

Financing Options for Importers

Financing options for importers in GCC countries include a variety of instruments and practices tailored to support the specific needs of businesses engaged in international trade. Here's an overview of some of the key financing options available:

Trade Credit: Suppliers may offer trade credit to importers, allowing them to pay for goods after a certain period, improving cash flow.

Bank Loans: Commercial banks in the GCC provide short-term loans to finance imports, often requiring collateral or a solid credit history.

Letters of Credit: A bank guarantee that ensures payment to the exporter upon fulfillment of shipment terms, reducing risk for both parties.

Export Credit Agencies (ECAs): ECAs offer government-backed loans, insurance, and guarantees to facilitate trade by mitigating risks such as non-payment and political instability.

Development Finance Institutions: These institutions provide support to small and medium-sized enterprises (SMEs) in the form of loans, lending programs, and insurance solutions.

Import VAT Deferral Regimes: Some GCC states may allow VAT-registered importers to defer the payment of import VAT, easing immediate financial burdens.

Invoice Factoring: Businesses can sell their accounts receivable to a factoring company at a discount, in exchange for immediate cash.

Islamic Finance: Sharia-compliant financial instruments, such as Murabaha and Ijara, are available for importers who wish to adhere to Islamic principles in their transactions.

It's important for businesses to carefully assess their financial needs and choose the most suitable option that aligns with their import activities and financial strategy. Consulting with financial experts and institutions that have experience in GCC trade can provide valuable insights and assistance in securing the right type of financing.

Chapter 7: Case Studies and Real-World Examples

Success Stories of Import Businesses

In this chapter, we delve into the inspiring success stories of import businesses that have thrived in the GCC's dynamic market. These real-world examples highlight the strategies, challenges, and triumphs of entrepreneurs and companies who have navigated the complexities of international trade within the GCC.

Case Study 1: Retail Revolution Discover how a retail giant expanded its operations across the GCC, capitalizing on the region's high per capita spending and strategic location to become a leading player in the market.

Case Study 2: Technological Triumph Learn about a tech startup that leveraged the GCC's push for digital transformation to introduce innovative products, resulting in rapid growth and regional recognition.

Case Study 3: Fashion Forward Explore the journey of a fashion brand that successfully entered the GCC market, adapting to cultural nuances and consumer preferences to establish a strong presence in the luxury segment.

Case Study 4: Healthcare Heroes Read about a healthcare company that identified a niche in the GCC's growing medical sector, providing high-quality products and services that aligned with the region's health initiatives.

Case Study 5: Food and Beverage Flourish See how a food and beverage importer tapped into the GCC's demand for quality and diverse culinary options, overcoming logistical challenges to satisfy the palate of a multicultural population.

Case Study 6: Building Bridges Examine how a construction materials business capitalized on the GCC's infrastructure boom, supplying essential products for major projects and becoming a trusted partner in development.

Conclusion

These case studies serve as a testament to the potential and opportunities that the GCC market holds for import businesses. They also provide valuable lessons on the importance of market research, cultural understanding, and strategic planning for success in this region.

By studying these examples, aspiring entrepreneurs and established businesses alike can gain insights into effective strategies for entering and thriving in the GCC import market.

GCC Imports Common Challenges and Solutions

Importing goods into GCC countries presents a unique set of challenges, but with the right strategies, these can be effectively managed. Here are some common challenges and their solutions:

Challenge 1: Navigating Regulatory Requirements

Solution: Stay informed about the GCC's import regulations, which are based on international benchmarks like Codex, GSO, OIE, and IPPC. Utilize the GCC Guide for Control on Imported Foods for comprehensive information.

Challenge 2: Market Competition

Solution: Understand the competitive landscape, which can be saturated and highly competitive. Offer unique products or services and establish a strong local presence to differentiate your business.

Challenge 3: Tariffs and Taxes

Solution: Be aware of tariffs and taxes, including the Common External Tariff (CET) and Value Added Tax (VAT), which can affect the cost of imports. Plan finances accordingly and consider the impact of free trade agreements.

Challenge 4: Supply Chain Complexities

Solution: Develop a robust supply chain with reliable suppliers and logistics partners. Consider diversifying your supply sources to mitigate risks.

Challenge 5: Cultural and Business Practices

Solution: Adapt to the local business culture, which values relationship-building. Understanding and respecting local customs can facilitate smoother transactions and negotiations.

Challenge 6: Financial and Currency Risks

Solution: Explore various financing options available for importers, such as bank loans, trade finance companies, and export credit agencies. Use financial instruments like letters of credit to secure transactions.

Challenge 7: Product Standards and Quality

Solution: Ensure that products meet GCC standards for quality and safety. Implement quality control systems and obtain necessary certifications to comply with regional regulations1.

By addressing these challenges with informed strategies and solutions, businesses can successfully import goods into GCC countries and capitalize on the opportunities within this dynamic market.

Lessons Learned from Experienced Importers

Experienced importers in GCC countries have shared valuable lessons that can benefit those looking to enter or expand their import operations in the region. Here are some key take ways:

Diversify Your Supply Chain: To mitigate risks, experienced importers recommend diversifying supply sources and not relying on a single country or supplier1.

Embrace Technology: Leveraging innovative technologies and e-commerce can streamline operations and enhance supply chain resilience.

Understand Local Regulations: A deep understanding of GCC customs and import regulations is crucial for smooth operations.

Build Strong Relationships: Establishing strong relationships with local partners, suppliers, and authorities can facilitate business processes and negotiations.

Plan for Logistics: Efficient logistics planning, including warehousing and transportation, is essential to ensure timely delivery and cost-effectiveness.

Focus on Quality: Maintaining high product quality and meeting GCC standards can set your business apart in a competitive market.

Financial Planning: Sound financial planning, including understanding tariffs, taxes, and currency risks, is vital for the sustainability of the import business.

Adapt to Market Needs: Being adaptable to the changing market needs and consumer preferences within the GCC can help capture new opportunities.

Cultural Sensitivity: Respecting and adapting to the local culture and business practices is important for long-term success.

Learn from Challenges: Use challenges as learning opportunities to improve and strengthen your business model.

These lessons underscore the importance of strategic planning, local knowledge, and adaptability in navigating the complexities of importing into the GCC market.

Importing cargo can be a rewarding venture if done correctly. With the knowledge and tools provided in this book, you'll be well-equipped to navigate the complexities of international trade and build a successful import business.

About the Author:

An industry expert with 18 years of experience in Quality Food safety and regulatory compliance in the supply chain field.

Useful Resources and Websites

For importing goods to GCC countries, several resources and websites can provide valuable information and guidance. Here are some useful resources:
1. **GCC Guide for Control on Imported Foods**: This guide by the General Authority of Customs provides principles and regulatory requirements for assuring the safety and suitability of shipments of imported food into the GCC countries[1]
2. **World Trade Organization - GCC Guide For Control On Imported Foods**: This document outlines the commitments of GCC member states to apply food control procedures based on the principle of severity of imported food and in line with expected consumer health and rights[2]
3. **GSO (GCC Standardization Organization)**: The GSO website offers access to all GCC food standards and technical regulations, which is crucial for ensuring compliance with regional requirements[3]
4. **GCC Statistical Center**: Provides foreign trade statistics, including trends and indicators of commodity trade between GCC countries and other nations, which can be useful for market analysis and decision-making[4]

These resources can help you navigate the complexities of importing goods to GCC countries, ensuring compliance with local regulations and standards. It's advisable to consult these resources regularly to stay updated on any changes or updates in the import procedures and regulations.

www.ingramcontent.com/pod-product-compliance
Lightning Source LLC
Chambersburg PA
CBHW070354230526
45471CB00006B/2562